Thank you

My heartfelt thanks to the following people, for this book wouldn't have happened without the contribution and support from many.

My beautiful Husband Rick for his unwavering encouragement and support – I love you, and my Mum Thea for her constant reminders to write this book for the past 3 years.

Jodie Nevid for pushing me and getting me out of my head and comfort zone.

To K for making this all possible.

Sally Heinrich for getting the book out of me and on paper. Your support and enthusiasm to me and other emerging writers is invaluable.

My inspirational teachers, James Porter and Basia Jedrzejczak, who encouraged my love of reading and public speaking. I only hope that one day I can guide and inspire others as you have done.

Amy and Ellie, for continuing to talk about our Brianna, and Brianna for being the love behind them. I love you forever and always.

MJP

For my Sister Brianna who lives in Heaven and for my Mummy Amy as well.
I love you.

Ellie

First published 2019
Text copyright © Michelle Jewels-Parsons
Illustrations copyright © Ellie Rose Hanham 2019
ISBN-13: 978-0-646-99915-9

Graphic design by Katherine Timotheou
Printed by Finsbury Green

www.thepresentbox.com.au

THE PRESENT BOX

A Collaboration of love and understanding by
Michelle Jewels-Parsons and her Niece Ellie Hanham

Today I feel different. I feel sad.
Not the sort of sad when I've done something wrong,
it's a different sad. My heart hurts today.

Someone I loved and cared about
who was very special to me has died.
Their body stopped working
and now I won't see them anymore.

I really liked seeing them
and spending time with them.
I loved their kisses and hugs and
they made my heart feel
warm and squishy.

In a few days, we are going somewhere to say goodbye. We have all been talking about the Goodbye Day. We talked about the Present Box, which I learnt is also called a coffin or casket.

This is a special box or basket you put someone in when they die.

You see when someone gives you a present, it's in a beautiful box with wrapping paper and ribbons. It's really pretty. Presents make me feel excited and I love getting presents.

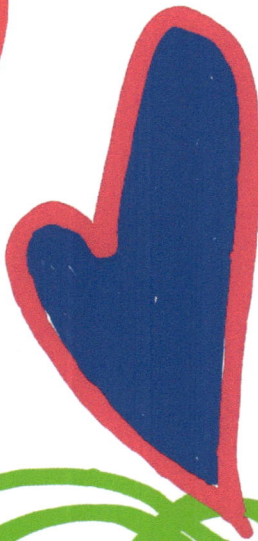

Well, the special person that
we're saying goodbye to was a
present to me because I loved them,
and they made me feel good.
They loved me too.

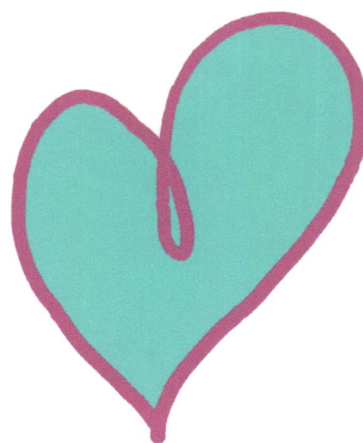

So for them we chose
a Present Box with pictures
of the beach on it, because
they loved the beach.
It always made them happy.

We'll cover the Present Box
with beautiful bright flowers because
they loved flowers too.

At the Goodbye Day (which some people call a Funeral) we will all say what we liked about them. Most of all we are going to say thank you for all their love and hugs and for being our friend.

We might see a movie with pictures
of them doing lots of things they loved.
I might be in them!

At the end of our together and goodbye time, I'll go up to the Present Box that my special friend is in. Then I have to say goodbye.

I'm going to whisper to the Present Box that I love them and that I'll miss them. To me, they were the *most* beautiful present of all.